# THE QUARANTINED TEEN *Life Interrupted*

## A Youth Anthology on the COVID-19 and Racism Pandemic of 2020

Copyright © 2020 Author Name

All rights reserved. No part of this book may be reproduced or transmitted in any form or by any means without written permission from the author.

T.A.L.K. Publishing
5215 North Ironwood Road, Suite 200
Glendale, WI 53217
talkconsulting.net

The Quarantined Teen
Life Interrupted
ISBN: 978-1-952327-17-9

# Dedication

This book is dedicated to the staff (past and present), interns and supporters of Lead2Change.

Your dedication to helping young people evolve into a thriving member of society with the skillset to succeed has made all of this possible.
To the students: Thank you! Thank you for showing us that you can, you have and you will continue to do so.

# THE QUARANTINED TEEN
# LIFE INTERRUPTED

ook Cover Design
concept Winner:
**Jaylon Arms**

# Acknowledgments

A special thank you to our partners that helped birth this project. Their partnership and funding provided an opportunity for students to engage in this process.

Lead2Change, Inc
Milwaukee Public Schools Contract Compliance Services Office of Accountability and Efficiency
Milwaukee Public Schools Partnership for the Arts and Humanities
Reasons For Hope MKE
T.A.L.K. Consulting, LLC

# Table of Contents

Foreword .................................................................................... 13

## The Quarantined Teen response to COVID ........................... 15

Isolated to Free COVID-19 ............................................................ 17
Dear COVID .................................................................................. 18
Letter to All .................................................................................... 19
Dear COVID 19 ............................................................................. 20
School Interrupted ......................................................................... 21
Focus on the Positive .................................................................... 22
Let's Talk ....................................................................................... 23
Anxiety .......................................................................................... 24
You Ruined Everything, At Least My Personal Life ..................... 25
I Have a Problem with You ........................................................... 27
Infatuated with Chaos ................................................................... 29
Senior Year Canceled .................................................................... 30
Dear Rona ..................................................................................... 31
Mask Off ....................................................................................... 32
I Was A Regular Person ................................................................ 33
I Don't Like You Anymore ............................................................ 34
I'm Surprised You're Still Here ..................................................... 36

## The Quarantined Teen response to RACISM ......................... 37

Biology of Hate ............................................................................. 39
The Hate You Give Is Scary ......................................................... 40
I've Heard So Much About You .................................................... 41
Baffled .......................................................................................... 43
Hiding in Plain Sight .................................................................... 44
Interesting Creature ...................................................................... 45
Stop This Pain .............................................................................. 46
I'm Just A Human ........................................................................ 47
You're A Terrible, Ugly, Awful Thing .......................................... 49
Race to the finish ......................................................................... 51
Shades of Color ........................................................................... 53
Hate ............................................................................................. 55

The Quarantined Teen: Meet the Authors ................................................. 59
The Quarantined Teen response to Life Interrupted ............................... 65
    Depression ................................................................................................ 67
    Future Me ................................................................................................. 68
    Broken Pain .............................................................................................. 69
    New Norms .............................................................................................. 70
    To My Future Children .......................................................................... 72
    Extra .......................................................................................................... 73
    Don't Forget Me ..................................................................................... 74
    Collection of the Things Missed Out On ............................................ 75
    Future Seniors ......................................................................................... 76
    Halted ....................................................................................................... 77
    Fear ........................................................................................................... 78
    Shaking ..................................................................................................... 80
    A Collective Voice .................................................................................. 82
    Emotions .................................................................................................. 83
The Quarantine Teen Journal Prompts .................................................... 85
    Our Parting Words ................................................................................. 90

# Foreword

"I can't breathe" are the words my brother whispered on the phone as he sat upright in a chair in his home. "I never felt pain like this before," he shared. As I sat on the line listening to him gasp for air, my eyes filled with tears. I never experienced nearly 6 feet of mass and strength in a place of such vulnerability. He had no control of this thing that welcomed itself into his life with the intent to harm.

I called 911 in an attempt to get him some help. Someone had to see and understand his state. With no breath, there is no life; with no life, there is no purpose. That is not how it was designed to be. To no surprise, the EMTs affirmed that he couldn't breathe, and like me, they felt helpless, not knowing what to do to fight this virus that had come with the intent of wiping out those it touched.

What do we do? The community is in an uproar from the effects of what appears to be an uncontrollable global pandemic. There is not enough money in the world that can wipe away the pain or economic hardship experienced by these individuals, families, and businesses all over the world. Not to mention the pain felt as another black man utters the phrase "I can't breathe." But this time, it is at the hands of a police officer. The world retaliates with global protests. Where do I fit? What am I to do? In my questioning of God, what I hear is a whisper that tells me to stay focused and that my purpose has not changed. How quickly I shifted.

For a moment, imagine being a teenager, and your world turns completely upside down due to a global pandemic. When schools closed, there was uncertainty about graduation and the next steps. Life was interrupted for millions of teens globally. Milwaukee was no different. The frustration, exhaustion, and just not knowing has caused a mix of emotions for teens as they navigate this experience without truly having an opportunity to discuss and, in some instances, understand how they feel.

This anthology gives voice to a perspective of what is occurring across the globe. What many students experienced and enjoyed during their senior year in high school was missed by many. I remember the summer before I was off to college. It was the summer of getting life in order as I transitioned to being an adult—so many beautiful memories of responsibility, goodbyes, and realizations. Unfortunately, millions of young people across the country now share a different experience.

These powerfully intense writings will provide insight while showcasing the incredible talent of these young authors. As you read, you will be catapulted into their journey as they reflect on the past, recant the present, and share what we must look forward to in the future. Ten and twenty years from now, they will unequivocally believe that every young person was created with purpose, and despite life's challenges, they still have to move towards the next steps to get there.

**Dionne Grayson,** Lead2Change, Inc

**THE QUARANTINED TEEN** *response to*
# COVID
# COVID
# COVID
# COVID
# COVID

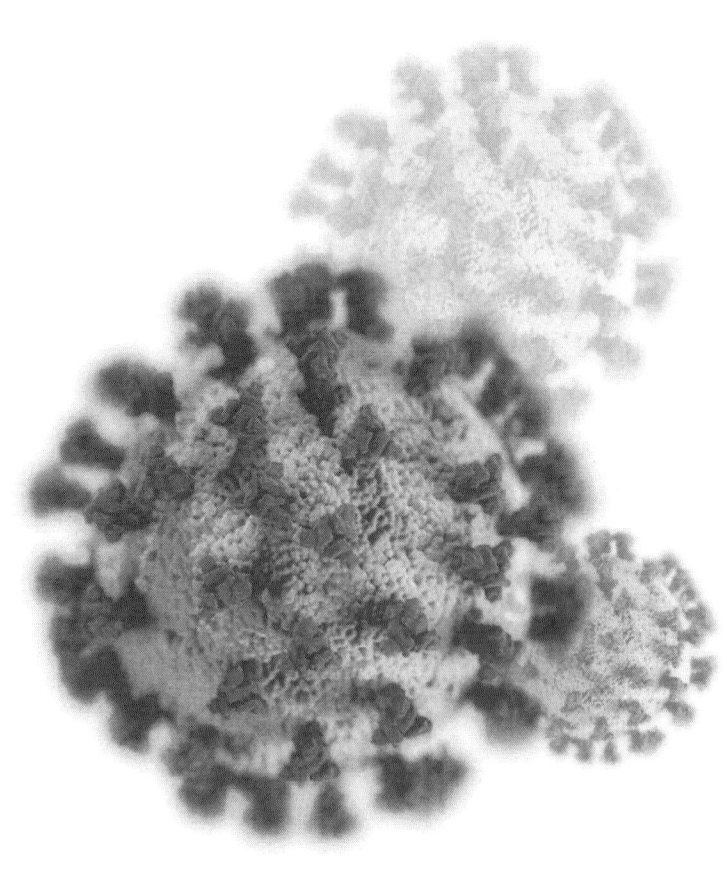

# Isolated to Free COVID-19

By: Darriunna Cole

At first, I was a homebody and didn't go anywhere or do anything, I just went to school and back home. I said no when my friends asked me to go places because I thought I saw them enough at school, and I isolated myself a lot. I really didn't know why, but I did. Now I'm regretting those moments when I could have spent time with my friends, and I chose not to. Now I'm starting to feel like I won't have moments like that anymore. COVID, you taught me many things but one thing you taught me is to live life to its fullest and to stop backing out on those little experiences that someday won't be anymore, which is what I'm feeling right now.

*The Quarantined Teen response to COVID*

# Dear COVID

By: Pa Kou Lee

It is **sad**,
**Hard**,
And **cruel** for you to come and
take away a loved one It's not
your fault but why are you still
continuing what you are doing
to people? Who cried no tears,
who stares towards you with
hatred So why do you still Insist
on creeping around? It's **cruel**
and **sad** to know that it's not your fault
And yet many blame you for taking
their loved one So answer my prayer
Why do you still keep Creeping
around every single person?
Are you not afraid of being called a virus?
Spreading sickness and people blaming you?

# Letter to All

### By: Stephon Ricks

Dear people,
It has been said
That he who has ears
Let him listen
And it must be mentioned
That he who has eyes
Let him see
We have been the "he" in this situation
We the He have done these things
Listening to thoughts of others
Some with a savory satisfaction
Others with a bitter sting
Witnessing all which transpires
From the near to the far
What happened to 2020's spring

It's a little overwhelming
Don't cha think
"It" as in everything
As in my life with yours
At least I imagine it would be
If I myself were to actually think
About what I have heard
And about what I have seen
About what's on the news
About "it"

# Dear COVID 19

## By: Anisha Prather

You've sparked the skies
and darkened our eyes
but yet we still can see

With a silent toll
of a human poll
we sit so recklessly

Figuring this out and
figuring that out
we feel like we oughta flee

But there's nowhere to go
in this fake filled snow so
Corona please let me be

# School Interrupted

By: Perrion Crawford

You will never know my pain. With school being interrupted due to you, it's making me miss the sports I love to do, such as football and track, but you will never know my pain. Not being able to play football hurts me more than playing football, and it makes me think, what if last season was my last season of ever playing. But yet again, you will never know my pain. I guess you will never know the pain and hurt of putting your all into something and for it to just be stripped away from you in a blink of an eye. Just not being able to experience the rush, the fun, the good sportsmanship from other teams, and even the bad sportsmanship hurts me deeply. But for the last time, you will never know my pain.

# Focus on the Positive

By: Temple Woods

Many people have suffered because of you. People have lost jobs, homes, and family members because of you. Many are fearful, confused, and feel hopeless. Millions have died because of you. I am thankful to say I am not one of those people. I have not suffered. My parents have not lost their jobs. We're not homeless, and I have not lost any family members. Honestly, I am not mad or angry at you. I am grateful to you. I mean, yes, there are things that I was looking forward to this year that couldn't happen, but I want to focus on the positive. I am grateful for the time I get to spend with my family. I am grateful that unlike other teens, the quarantine didn't necessarily affect me the way that it did others. I believe being this way because of homeschooling. I have been homeschooled since 6th grade, and at this point, I have gotten used to working independently. Being quarantined wasn't that bad for me, either. I was pretty much a home-body before this anyway. It's also allowed me to gain a few hobbies, like playing video games. I feel like most people are choosing to look at the negative right now because it's easier than facing your own personal issue. Don't you know that focusing on the negative won't solve anything? Being stuck in that cycle of self-pity will get you nowhere. The more time you spend feeling sorry for yourself is less time spent working to solve the problem. You have all this time to fix the issue you have been pushing off until now, USE IT. We don't know when we will get this time again. There is too much negativity already in the world for us to wallow in self-pity. We should be focusing on the positive aspects of our lives right now, like the times we all have with our family, and birthdays we have celebrated through Zoom. Don't let this disease stop you from having a positive outlook on your life and the moments you are creating now, even when negativity surrounds us. Besides, what a great story we'll tell generations after this.

Sincerely,

A Quarantined Teen

# Let's Talk

## By: Tyrone Harper

Hello, COVID

I'm going to be honest, you've helped me a little bit. The closure of schools has helped me realize that I was afraid to start college and overcome that fear. You've also given me the chance to reflect on my life choices. Although, killing that many people is unforgivable. Because of you, I couldn't say goodbye to my classmates in person, even if I didn't want to. You've locked us all away in our homes, keeping us from our daily lives. You even try to be slick by not affecting the youth so that they would spread you to the older generation. Honestly, you're trying to be one of the big pandemics, like smallpox. You may have started this pandemic, but you can rest assured...We will end it.

Get off my planet

The Quarantined Teen response to COVID

# Anxiety

### By: Darriunna Cole

All this anxiety and fear built up in my head

Constantly asking myself will this ever end

Trying to do everything in my power to keep you from getting in

But how can I really? I can't feel you, can't see you, can't talk to you but I wish I could

I guess we can say you're kinda in control, but you don't have a single target, everyone is your target

You may separate us, break us, kill us, you might have even changed us but you didn't make us

It's crazy how you can start in one place and reach thousands of people from all over the world

It's like our world evolved around you

# You Ruined Everything, At Least My Personal Life

By: Jacqueline Oliva-Jacobo

You ruined everything. And yet, at least in my personal life, you may have done some good. But don't you dare think that just because you may have spared me some pain doesn't make up for the pain you've caused to millions. You wrecked the world and destroyed my final year in high school. Although compared to the whole world, me missing out on the last three months of school doesn't seem all that important. But it was important to me.

It was my final year of high school. We were just about to get to the fun, end of the year things every senior does. We were so close. So close. The news of how you were going around the world spread like wildfire. But life here continued as normal. We didn't think things would get worse.

How wrong we were.

The last "normal" day for me was March 13th. It was a regular day for me. I was going to school, helping my Art Teacher in the Art room, talking to my middle school students, etc. The topic of the day was you. With discussions about if school would be canceled or how bad things would get. Everyone thought that there was no way school would shut down. We'd go off on spring break and come back, and everything would be better. My middle school students were helping me mix clay and talking about you.

Overshadowing you was the talk of how excited they were for a trip to the roller-skating rink that morning. I paid some of them for their hard work helping with the clay and couldn't wait for Monday to roll around so they could tell me how the trip went. The day continued with whispers about you. It ended, and I went home, only to find out hours later the news about how school was shut down. How? I thought. It seemed unreal. An extended break from school! I looked on the bright side. I can play some video games I've been meaning to play, sleep in, etc.

But while I was happily locked inside, you were destroying livelihoods and lives.

It was one thing after another. *Total shutdowns worldwide!* The number of deaths is getting higher and higher. *Shortages and limits of supplies and food.* My parents were essential workers, putting them and myself at risk for you.

No return to school for the rest of the school year. Which meant my senior year activities were erased, just like that. 13 years of school, and I can't even have a wonderful and big celebration with my family, celebrating my grand accomplishment. No walking across the stage in my gown and cap (now what do I do with it?), no final in-person goodbyes. No hugs, no grand gesture of love I was going to do for my crush. No senior week activities. Goodbye breakfast bar, senior prank, roller-skating, bowling, and in-person college decision day. No seeing my middle school students again. No goodbyes to them, and no goodbyes to the school in person one last time.

But you did one good thing.

My father had an internal issue, one that would've happened regardless of you. He was sent to the ER alone for days, recovering from surgery. It happened the weekend my graduation was initially supposed to be. He would've missed it had it still happened as intended. Do not get me wrong, I would've rather you never occurred in the first place. Even if it meant my father couldn't see me. Things just ended up this way. It was one little spark of good amongst the millions of unforgivable things you did.

It's selfish of me to complain about what you ruined for me when you ruined very little, at least compared with what you've done to others.

You've killed people. Thousands of lives that would've stayed alive longer had it not been for you. You've ruined jobs and stuck millions in unemployment. You've ruined so much for the world for the foreseeable future. You've caused panic and mayhem. You did all this and for what!?!? WHAT DO YOU GAIN FROM THIS?!? THE WORLD WILL NOT RECOVER FOR A LONG TIME, AND THE WORLD WILL *BE FOREVER CHANGED* IN MANY WAYS BECAUSE OF YOU. ARE YOU PROUD OF WHAT YOU DID? ARE YOU HAPPY?? ARE YOU SATISFIED?? IF SO, CAN YOU PLEASE STOP ALL THIS?!

Please.

It's stupid to try and bargain with you. I can't bargain with you. No one can. We can only try and reason and contain you until a better solution comes along. I can try to reason with you. Emphasize on try. Please go away soon. Please disappear by next year. The world can't sustain life like this.

But you won't listen.

And you'll never listen.

You only infect and kill.

# I Have a Problem with You

## By: Dianyeliz Garcia

Hey, how have you been? I saw you came to town, and a lot of people do not like you. They talk about how you are a pandemic and that you just kill people. You attack the lungs and just kill. I mean, I have a problem with you, but it is not like you are picking and choosing who you are going to affect. It is not like you are police officers who racially profile us, kill us because of our race, and kill us with malicious intentions. It's like you have a superiority complex, and you kill the very people who you are supposed to protect. I heard since most of the world was in quarantine, that you fixed some of the ozone layers. Also, pollution decreased in the air. It sucks you have to kill people and steal moments we can never get back, but I get it. You are just doing your job to survive. We see you as a killer, but we are trying to kill you too. Does that make us any different?

Maybe, we as the human race are a pandemic to this world. We are viruses, diseased to the ones who are just trying to survive. We kill and kill but we hate you for killing us. We even kill each other but WHO decides what global epidemic and a public safety hazard are. Yet, some people are pleading for their countries to create reform in their government. That is not a public safety concern, I guess. The world is just, I have no words.

Corona, you took a lot of opportunities from me. I couldn't walk across the stage; my parents did not see me walk across the stage to get my diploma. However, I do not care about these lost moments anymore. I learned to value my life and learn that every moment counts. It sucks for my parents not to see me walk across the stage, but it will be worse if my parents could not ever see me walk again, period. I, Dianyeliz, thank you. Not everyone will understand why I thank you, but you allow me to put circumstances into perspective. I would rather breathe with healthy lungs than have a police officer on my neck for 8 minutes.

## The Quarantined Teen response to COVID

I would rather play outside in my neighborhood than get shot in my stomach twice. I would rather wish my mother could hear how much I love her before it is too late. You see, Corona, I am not scared of you. I am more scared to live in a country that values goods and services more than my black brothers and sisters. I am scared to live in a country that imprisons children and sexually abuse them because they are "illegals." I am scared to live in a country that allows an orange bigot to run our country. I am scared to be scared because it allows my foes to have power over me.

As I yearn for my freedom, not just from you, I hope that I will see it soon.


Sincerely,


A concerned citizen

# Infatuated with Chaos

By: Kenya Handy

Although you didn't change much in my life, I am still very upset about all the lives you took. You even affected some of my friends. Why did you come in and make things on earth even more complicated than they already are? I am not only upset with you but the people that won't let you go. They won't wear a simple mask. Why is it so hard for people to listen to one simple command to save the earth? It's like they're in love with you. They are infatuated with the chaos you have brought to us. It doesn't make any sense. Hopefully, people get their act together so that things will go back to normal.

## Senior Year Canceled

By: Jeremiah Lipscomb

It's hard to look forward to a promising future when your future doesn't seem promising. You allowed your corruption to spread around the world. It ruined the lives of many, including mine.

My senior year, canceled. Now it seems as if my college freshman year will be as well. It's so annoying that others aren't complying with the safety precautions. They don't wear a mask because they think they're invincible. They go to parties because they prioritize fun over safety.

America opens up the economy putting many lives in danger. These are prime examples of how completely ignorant America is. I wish people would be safe instead of putting their lives on the line. You don't know how serious everything is until you or your family are harmed. As you continue your reign of terror on the lives of many and manipulate the minds of many industries, I will remain humble and avoid succumbing to America's ignorance.

## Dear Rona

By: Stephon Ricks

I guess you caught me a bit by surprise
Ya know,
Off guard, slackin',
Unaware and unprepared
Through the eyes of victims
You must've seen that I wasn't ready
I mean I could've sworn I was
Legs planted and eyes steady
But nah, I wasn't
I wasn't prepared for your impact
And the mark you'd leave upon your wake
I didn't expect the toll onto humanity
With the constant rise in death rate
I didn't know my reality would change so much
Though I did enjoy that early summer break
And I never would've figured
Buying hand sanitizer would become such a headache
But like I say
It is what it is
And I can't make life what it ain't
All I can do is
Stay focused
Grab my bearings
And keep my head on straight

# Mask Off

### By: Mordechai Tinney

Do you know how much damage you've done? I doubt it.
You've left hundreds of thousands of people with grief
And millions more with fear
Merely in the U.S.
Holding true to tradition, America First.

You've never said a word,
Yet you have been able to make so many things clear
Revealing that the real sickness is not in you,
But has been a part of us for so long.
The willingness to blame,
The eagerness to ignore when things are not "our problem"

But don't feel bad, it's not your fault
You opened our eyes and let us see our world for what it truly is
Hateful.
Selfish.
Rooted.
You took off your mask and
Left tradition in danger.

# I Was A Regular Person

## By: Jasen Moore

I was a regular person at high school
I was ready for the football season
but you took it and created your own season
It was going to be my first time in pads
I thought I was going to juke and break ankles all season
little did I know you were coming at me like a five-star running back to break mine
you selfishly took the lives of many so when you die,
I won't take pity.

## I Don't Like You Anymore

### By: Pa Kou Lee

My life

**Before** you came into my life
I was always that girl who goes to school
Always trying to find excuses to run away from my struggles
Always making sure everything was excellent
Always trying to not make trouble

**Two weeks**
I've known you for two weeks
Still, it was like a dream to be away from stress in school
It was stressful, painful, but I had to persevere through it all
I had to because I wanted
To achieve greater goals

**A month**
I've known you for a month now
It was all fun and games until somebody got hurt
You're making my life harder than it was before
This is my punishment for wanting to have a day off of school
This is my punishment for trying to run away from my stress
I should have faced it but I didn't

**Four months**
I've known you for four months
I'm tired of you
I'm slowly going crazy just by the thoughts of you
It's exhausting to be cooped up in this house

I don't want to know you anymore
But yet you never went away

I don't like you anymore, **COVID**
You took away my happiness
My dreams and hopes
You shatter the beautiful scenery that I could've experienced
Walking across that stage
You took away my mom's dream of watching me graduate
You took away the times I could have spent
Hanging out with my friends

I don't like you anymore, **COVID**

## I'm Surprised You're Still Here

By: Jaylon Arms

I'm surprised that you're still here if I'm really honest. If we had more control over this situation, we probably would've gotten rid of you by this point. I wish it would've gone that way because you've pretty much made everyone crazy. To be fair, though, you're only something that we've seen on TV and video games, something that can affect the entire country and even the world. You have put people all over the world in a pretty stressful situation for the last few months. You got people all over the world in a state of panic and stress that I can't describe. However, I don't think that you're too bad. You helped us improve our lives and see the wrong in us in such a way that I don't think that we could even see. You made work from home a thing and the new norm but made us see Racism, something ugly in us that we've had for a long time. That's all in the past, though, and personally, I'm looking towards the future—a future where you don't belong.

**THE QUARANTINED TEEN** *response to*
# RACISM
RACISM
RACISM
RACISM
RACISM

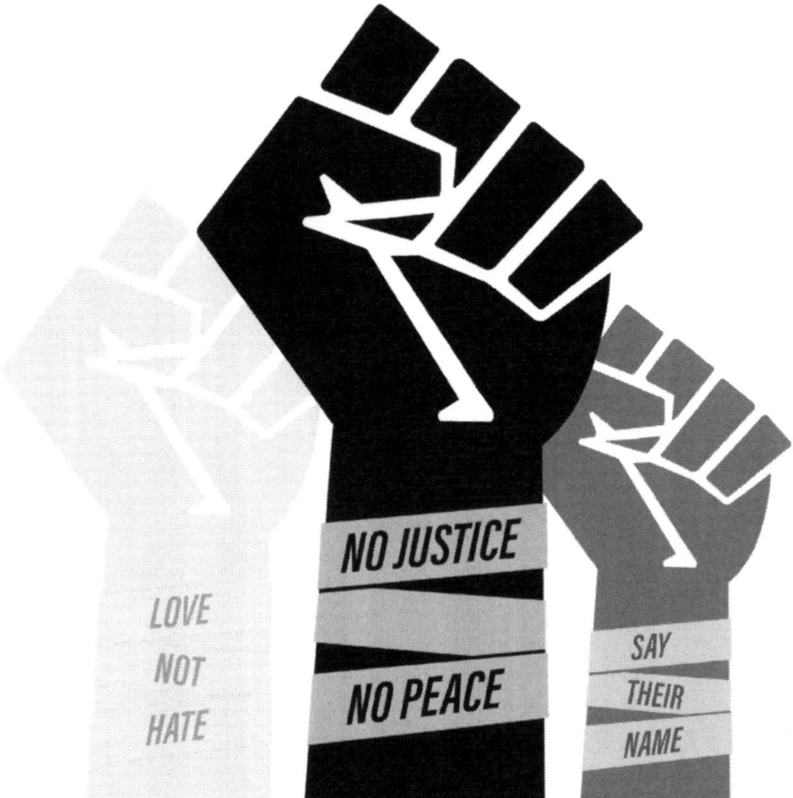

LOVE
NOT
HATE
NO JUSTICE
NO PEACE
SAY
THEIR
NAME

# Biology of Hate

By: Mordechai Tinney

Hatred is Biological
Its preference Genetic
Grandparents teaching parents teaching children, how to hate
Unintentional sometimes, racist nonetheless

Denial of Hate

Hatred is Denying
Deciding that someone's pain doesn't exist
Daily compromises unseen, invalid
Or Deflection and Pity with no course of action

Humanity of Hate

Hatred is Human
The chance for power
Rooted in how we live
Traditions so powerful and encompassing

America is Hatred
Like an illness, we are sick
Hate allowed to quietly live, not letting others live quietly.
Like a sickness, we need help or we are doomed to perish.

## The Hate You Give Is Scary

By: Reginald Johnson Jr

Hello Racism, you killed so many people. It's sad that so many people still follow you. I don't know who created you because you are really evil. You make lots of different people upset, and I want to change this mindset you put in people, and it's only getting worse. And now this BLM campaign is going on all over the world, and it shows to this day that people are so stupid and fail to realize that *all* lives matter will only happen if *black* lives are in it. To end someone's life then boast about it like you that guy signing skittles like it's a joke. You got people walking up to Zimmerman like he saved his community. Don't make me laugh because we been laughed at, persecuted, and mocked with this solution to find Racism. It's like we are in a wild goose chase, but we need to slow down and realize it's the white man's race. We have been pushing our limits for centuries.

I remember what you did to our people. Throwing us on a ship, whip us, rape us. Racism, if you were a person, I would kill you slowly because you make me sick. You, trying to say sorry for slavery, is unbelievable. This has been going for so long in time, and it still happens today, 155 years later, we are still getting killed. How are we supposed to forget that?? Forget you and the people that follow you. I'm tired of this hate because it makes me angry. Pushing you away is the only way to go. Pushing our weight around will only make this boat sink. Evil is in you, that's why we have to change the way you think.

Sincerely,

BLACK COMMUNITY

# I've Heard So Much About You

## By: Stephon Ricks

I've heard much about you
And honestly I don't have much to say
You're known as a concept of the past
Yet also a constant of the present
You've destroyed the lives of many
Killing the freedom of their offspring
You've created a cycle of hatred
Disregarding its everlasting consequences
You've preserved the ways of days past
Moving men to hang others from twisted twine
And while I've never been the type to point fingers
I must be upfront
It is your fault that I question
the morality of each person with skin which contrasts mine
But you know
I guess I shouldn't blame you
At least not as much anyways
You did not spawn yourself
But merely the creation of bitter men
You did not employ yourself
But merely used as a tool of oppression
And you did not permit your striving existence
But merely never left alone by the masses
You see
It's not about you

## The Quarantined Teen response to RACISM

It's...
And regardless of what happens
I'm sure you'll be here when I die
But like I said
I don't have much to say

# Baffled

By: Temple Woods

It baffles me that you still exist, that there are people out there that hate others because of the color of their skin. Some think black people are less than human. They believe our lives don't matter as much as theirs or at all. Then there are the people that say they aren't racist or don't *hate* black people, but still call the police when they feel like a black person is threatening them. Finally, you have the government and policing system built on white supremacy. I mean, come on it's 2020 shouldn't we all know that no man or woman is better than the other. It's like some people don't get the concept of treating people the way they want to be treated. No, that's not true; they do get the concept but are choosing to only apply it to themselves or people they consider human. That's why you're still here. They're choosing to ignore the systems you have put in place. The stigmas in our governments, police departments, schools, and communities. The stigmas and stereotypes in our television shows, movies, books, music, our culture, and society in general. Choosing to believe the saying, "Black Lives Matter," contradicts "All Lives Matter," when black lives should be a part of the "All" in "All Lives Matter." Choosing to believe that police brutality on black people is over-exaggerated because "white people get killed more often by police". Of course, that will happen- white people, as of 2020, makeup 49% of the population in America compared to the population of black people, which is 13%.

Criticizing me for bigger lips, wider hips, and darker complexion but goes to a plastic surgeon or tanning salon to get the same thing. Calling my braids "unprofessional," but when you wear it it's "for fun" or "it's just hair"—calling my big brothers thugs unless they're entertaining you. Spending weeks talking about American colonization, but forgetting to mention that this is the same land you stole from the Indigenous people and ignore the fact that slavery is just as much American history as anything in those textbooks. Celebrating Independence Day every year, but if we mention slavery and/or segregation, we should "forget something the happened in the past." They're choosing to turn a blind eye to the blatant Racism displayed every day in America, so they can still live comfortably. The one thing we as humans have in common is our free will and when there are people that choose to be racist or ignorant at the expense of others...how can we make change? That is why you still exist and that's why you'll never leave.

The Quarantined Teen response to RACISM

# Hiding in Plain Sight

Mordechai Tinney

You seem to enjoy hiding in plain sight. Disguised in white clothes and ivory sheets. I used to not see you. I was told I didn't need to see you. Told you were none of my concern. So you slithered under my radar and hid. You were allowed to do so. You were obligated to do so.

To me, I thought you carried nothing more than a stick, one that a small child would be so proud to find. One that, in that child's hand, was harmless. That stick, too, was a disguise. But rather a Gatling gun that will level a city, a town, a community.

We found you wandering: seemingly unintentional. Little did I know, every step you took was calculated and measured to cause the most strife, it was necessary. Under a guise of rarity, I assumed you were small. But the only version I saw of you was not your true self, just the most extreme. Murders invoked through hate, lynching's erupting from nothing more than a *misstep*, a *mistake*, a *specific* mistake—the mistake of being born with darker skin.

A child is a threat, with a toy gun and dark skin.
An EMT is a threat, in her own house and dark skin.
A young man is a threat with a facemask and dark skin.

Life is not lived in the big events, but rather the small acts of prejudice every day. The glares, the walk-arounds, the purse-clutches. Fractions of humanity denied is humanity denied nonetheless. And it took so long for me to see.

## Interesting Creature

By: Jaylon Arms

I'm going to be real with you. You're such an interesting creature to me. It's not that I think you're special in any way. It's just that despite our best efforts to get rid of you, you've still managed to stick around for all these years. You managed to become a part of life. Affecting people of different races for way too many years, and I feel like I know why too. I think it's because people like you refuse to accept other races. They refuse to accept that all races should have the same amount of freedom as any other race, and most importantly, the refusal to go away, knowing you're not wanted around anymore. That's not even the worst part either; the worst part isn't that you should've been gone ever since the civil rights act, or that you're in every single generation or the fact that you make others feel ashamed to be themselves. It's the fact that you're here. The so-called "Land of the Free." The land with freedom of speech but no freedom if you're a specific race. The land where clear discrimination between races still exists despite all we've done to stop it. So Racism, do us a favor and get out. Get out so that we can be free and live together in peace, and have the unity and freedom that the U.S. is supposed to stand for.

The Quarantined Teen response to RACISM

## Stop This Pain

By: Anisha Prather

History repeats itself
for better or for worse,
but with you around it feels more like a curse

Hurting me and hurting them
we can't breathe any more
Nowadays it seems like everyone's
tryna break down my door

We can't get some rest
we can't get some sleep,
cause all you do is cut so deep

Stop this pain you've caused my chest
I don't even wear a vest
I'm trying to do my best
you overly obnoxious jest

## I'm Just A Human

### By: Pa Kou Lee

Everywhere I go and everything I do
People are always calling me a virus
Even though it came as a shock for me as well

Yet they have no problem blaming me
Just because I have a different skin color
Just because I don't speak their language
They think they have the obligation
To blame me just because I'm different

Everywhere I go and everything I do
People are always looking at me strange
Calling me a virus
Accusing that I brought America to an end
Making me a murderer when I have not killed anyone
I deny everything yet I was yelled at for lying
When in truth I had done nothing wrong

I ignore yet I got pulled hard
Making my life harder than what it should be

Just because my skin color is different
I avoid the situation yet was called a virus
When I was trying hard to protect myself
From the cold

The people ignore my plea
That I'm not the one

## The Quarantined Teen response to RACISM

Who brought this virus over to America
That I'm just a human being like everyone else in the world
Protecting myself like everyone else does

But they overlooked and rejected my plea and insisted that I brought over the deadly virus to kill people
That I have bloody hands colliding with the evil that I'm working for the devil

I refuse all the accusations
but nothing comes through those thickheaded people
Who love to accuse and abuse
people of color

How would they feel
if they were accused and abused the same way?
How would they like it if someone
called them something they are not?
How would they understand my struggles
When they didn't go through what I experienced

# You're A Terrible, Ugly, Awful Thing

By: Jacqueline Oliva-Jacobo

You're a terrible thing. You know that? You're a terrible, ugly, awful thing. I've experienced you before, so I know firsthand how disgusting you are.

Growing up in a mostly Hispanic community, at first, I never did. My first school was majority Hispanic, and so were my classmates. Once I moved to a majority white and black school and encountered more of the world, I got to know you better. As one of the only Hispanic kids, I was constantly asked if I was here legally or if I could speak Spanish. I was asked countless upon countless times to say things in Spanish. People would ask me if I had tacos every night for dinner.

You didn't just impact me, but you've affected others. My sister pretends to be native American while out and about for fear of how people would react to her being Mexican. I've seen several videos of you infecting others, and those people yell and scream and hit my people for being themselves. They blame my people for taking their jobs, for not speaking English, and telling us to go home. They're spurred on by the racist president at the head of America currently. They hate us so much that they try to build a wall, thinking that just because the president is racist, they too, can be openly racist. They call us beaners, wetbacks, etc. They try to make us feel shame in our culture, our motherland, and who we are. They have an entire organization dedicated to finding and forcefully taking us, when we only tried to make a living here—those who have come for a better life for our families, for those we love, for better chances, for more opportunities. We do what anyone who wants to live a good life for our loved ones and us.

We're HUMANS.

Why do you infect people to hate not only us but others of color? Why does it matter what race we are? Why does the color of our skin matter at all? Why can't some people look past the color of others' skin?

I just don't get why you exist??? Without you, the world would be a much better place.

With you, the people of the world think it's fine to put children in cages, separated from their families in absolutely terrible conditions like they're dogs! Oh wait, I'm sorry, some people in this world treat dogs, literal animals, better than Mexican children. They treat them like humans; meanwhile, they treat the children just like animals.

But it's not just my race that suffers because of you. It's pretty much everyone that isn't white. We all get treated like "fashion", or a Halloween costume or animals.

WE ARE HUMAN BEINGS.

Why can we be treated as such?

## Race to the finish

By: Dianyeliz Garcia

For my life is on the
l-i-n-e
I chase the reform
To bloom
{IN} to a beautiful flower
For my colors are
Vibrant
Like my
SKIN
Bright with melanin with a shade of cream
I was stolen
Taken on a ship
Exported like cattle
I was created by sin
Gold, Gold, Glory
For the white man
In the name of God
I hope God forgives you

MY PEOPLE
Were slaughtered
Will, you not take accountability?
Stole our people from the motherland and exported them to la isla
Yo soy boricua no estoy Puertorriqueña.
I am not no "Porto Rican"
Yo soy boricua como el coqui dentro de mi corazón

### The Quarantined Teen response to RACISM

We are reborn...
To the Tainos...
To my African ancestors...
I will prove right by you
To the Spaniards...
Apologize.
For my people were not the ones to colonize
And I despise
Your very existence

# Shades of Color

By: Olivia R. Clark

LIGHT-BRIGHT, YELLOW, WHITE, and LIGHTSKIN, are the names given to me from everyone in life associated with you. They treat me differently, no matter where I go, but no race will love me for me. Not even my own BLACK COMMUNITY. I thought we would have unity. It's hard enough being a `black female in this world, but it seems like it's a dream world. Sometimes it's good times, and sometimes it's bad times. My dad, a beautiful Black King, had it really hard though, he was born in 1950 when the Civil Rights era began. He's a "light-bright" too; it's something we both go through, except his era was harder than mine. He grew up in Pittsburgh, Pennsylvania, the "ghetto," but he was the only light skin one of 10 kids. He was bullied all his life because of you, but I guess this was just the start of your plan.

My mom went through a similar thing; she was born in the 1960s. One thing, she's darker than us but is as beautiful as the Springtime and is my beautiful Black Queen. My mom has two other sisters and is the middle child. ,. They were all bullied each because of their skin tones. My mom's oldest sister was darker but not as much as her; they would say my aunt stayed in the oven the right amount of time. As for my mom, they would say she should've stayed in the oven longer. But my mom's younger sister is dark skin, and they told her she stayed in the oven way too long. I never thought my parents experienced what I went through right now. Nevertheless, I have a beautiful family; don't get me wrong it's just that I feel that I don't fit in at all. It's okay, though, because I still love them.

My family has become more diverse over the years, I have a Vietnamese/Black sister named Misty, who was born during the Vietnam war, and is married to a white man named Chris. My dad met Misty's mom when he was serving in the Vietnam war, and she got pregnant, but before Misty was even born, the war was over. My dad came home, not knowing if the child was a boy or girl. When Misty was born, she went through so much because she is a BLACK American soldier's child. So she and her mom were treated differently. Misty and her mom left Vietnam and went to Westminster, California. Westminster is basically where all the Vietnamese refugees traveled during the 1980s. Misty eventually did better, but she had a terrible car accident where she went into a coma for almost a year. They were ready to pull the plug, and then suddenly, she woke up. Because Misty was in a horrible car accident, she suffered a brain injury and had to learn everything all over again. Chris and Misty were very good friends. When she finally woke up, Chris was by her side, helping her until she got better. This formed a bond between them, and when she got better, they were married in 2008. Now, they, too, have their own blended family. To add to the diversity, my brother is marrying a white woman. All of this is fine with me because it's good to have another point of view of life and how each of them came up. Despite you, we can talk about racial problems without arguing about it. It's odd but strange to say I love how diverse we are.

I've talked about all my other family members' experiences with you, but I only told you a little about what you put me through. Where do I even begin to tell you, let's start with me, finally starting school. I went to the same school as my brother because it was close to our old house, so it was walking distance. Before my brother went off to high school, his friends would always call me the odd one out because I was lighter than my other siblings. My brother would tell them don't say that to me, even though he sometimes did the same. I heard words like "joke" "Casper", "whitey", "white man", and more. Once my brother left, I was still being picked on by everyone in school, literally every day, until I was picked to go to Golda Meir in 3rd grade. I thought you wouldn't have followed me there, but boy was I wrong, you were there for it all. I was still being bullied based on the shade of my skin. I've been at Golda since I was in 3rd grade. They added on a high school, so you can say I spent the majority of my school life there. When I started dating, I had a feeling you would still be here, but I didn't know you would affect my dating life. The majority of the people I've dated only dated me because they liked that I was light skin not because they liked me for me, they thought I was mixed with something else other than black or would assume I'm white. You made my life so hard and still are, but I think you are enjoying this honestly because it seems when I'm down, and at my lowest point, it looks like you just love to see me hurt and down.

I have a question for you old friend. Why must you torture me so? What have I done to you that made you want to hurt me mentally and emotionally? But since you probably won't give me an answer, let me just inform you on something about me, I'm still a strong, beautiful black goddess making her way through this place we call home. I will keep pushing through what you continuously keep putting me through. And when I have kids and **my** *own* family, just know I will prepare them for you and even what you will put them through. So thank you. Thank you for showing me your true colors and showing me how my black is beautiful. I'll see you later, old friend.

*Love Always,*

Olivia R. Clark

# Hate

### By: Tyrone Harper

To Racism,

You disgust me. All you've done is drive the human race apart. Because of you, this has been exposed, America was created with Racism as one of its roots. You've built a country on the backs of unwilling slaves. Slaves that were only there because you made people believe that they were above them. You made them seem like cattle for others to abuse. I look at the flag that you help to create, red, and blue with white stars. I see the white stars that my ancestors followed to experience the blue skies of freedom, willing to shed the red blood that they bear on their backs from the strikes of hate. Now, when I walk down the street, past someone who doesn't look like me, I have to consider if they are friends with you. In the past, you were upfront and proud of yourself until the black community pushed back against you. This isn't the only example of people pushing against you, but it's the one that's close to me. Nowadays, you lurk in the shadows. You talk behind closed doors. Because now, if one of your puppets gets caught, we'll burn it alive. Long story short, I hate you. Scratch that. The things that you've encouraged other people to do are evil and ill-mannered, but I'll forgive you. You were born from hate. I don't want to be responsible for spawning something like you. Just leave and don't come back.

Sincerely,

Tyrone

**THE QUARANTINED TEEN:** *Meet the*
# Authors
Authors
Authors
Authors
Authors

Pictured left to right: Row (1) Anisha, Darriunna, Dianyeliz - Row (2) Jaqueline, Jaylon, Jeremiah – Row (3) Kenya, Keone, Mordechi, - Row (4) Olivia, Pa Kou, Reginald, - Row (5) Stephon, Temple, Tyrone

## Anisha Prather

Lights, camera, animation! Anisha Prather is a Junior in high school and an aspiring Animator. With a talent for drawing and an eye for visual design, Anisha has aspirations to one day work on her own animated series. Inspired by the art of creation and innovation, Anisha is well on her way to manifesting her dreams.

This anthology means a lot to Anisha, and she is hopeful that it will bring people together.

## Darriunna Cole

With a heart filled with many goals and desires, Darriunna Cole is interested in pursuing a career in Nursing. Entering her senior year, Darriunna is committed to achieving an outstanding academic year. Since participating in Dream.Explore.Build., Darriunna has gained more confidence and is ready to go after her dreams boldly.

Darriunna never imagined that she would contribute words that would be published in a book. She is excited to be a part of this anthology.

## Dianyeliz Garcia

Dianyeliz Garcia is passionate about helping people grow and develop healthy coping mechanisms. She is also committed to understanding the thoughts and feelings of others. This passion has led Dianyeliz to pursue a career in Psychology. Dream.Explore.Build., has allowed Dianyeliz to gain more connections in her desired career, as she is currently working with aspiring psychiatrists in their final years of medical school. Dianyeliz will attend UW-Madison in the fall as a freshman. She also plans to attend graduate school. With a boost in confidence, Dianyeliz is well on her way to achieving her goals.

It has always been a goal of Dianyeliz to become a published author. She is excited that her dream has come true.

## Jacqueline Oliva-Jacobo

Helping the next generation express themselves through art brings an indescribable joy for Jacqueline Oliva-Jacobo. As an aspiring Art Teacher, Jacqueline utilized several career exploration opportunities, including an internship in illustration, to lead her down the right path. Jacqueline looks forward to studying Art Education at Mount Mary University in the fall. She is most appreciative of her passionate spirit and willingness to put her heart and soul into anything in her path.

For Jacqueline, participating in this anthology means being a part of history. This will be something she can look back later on in life and have those thoughts and emotions rush back to her.

## Jaylon Arms

For someone who values creative freedom, Jaylon Arms naturally gravitated towards a career in graphic design. Dream.Explore.Build. , served as a gateway for Jaylon to acquire a more in-depth understanding of graphic design and the skills and education required. Jaylon is entering his Junior year, and Jaylon's focus will be on working towards his academic and career goals. One thing's for sure, Jaylon's creativity will open many doors for him.

Participating in this anthology means that Jaylon can help make a difference in the world and be a part of history.

## Jeremiah Lipscomb

With a passion for software technology and coding language, Jeremiah Lipscomb looks forward to pursuing a promising career in Software Engineering. To launch his career, Jeremiah will attend UW-Madison in the fall. Jeremiah has thoroughly enjoyed networking with professionals and developing soft skills through Dream.Explore.Build. In the future, Jeremiah looks forward to developing innovative software for electronics or appliances. Dream.Explore.Build. has taught Jeremiah that most opportunities come to individuals who search for them. With perseverance, Jeremiah is determined to grab every opportunity in his path.

Known for not being the center of attention, Jeremiah is ready to step into the light for a cause that he really cares about with this anthology.

## Kenya Handy

Enamored by animals and their anatomy, Kenya Handy aspires to become a Veterinarian and pursue this career path when she enters college this fall. Kenya is appreciative of her experience in Dream.Explore.Build. Not only has the program helped her develop business etiquette, but it has also encouraged her to dream and never stop pursuing her goals.

This anthology means a lot to Kenya, and she is ready to share her feelings and experiences with her peers and the world.

## Keone Westfall

One thought of the universe and all its complexity, and Keone Westfall is in love. Entering his senior year, Keone plans to study Theoretical Physics in college. Through Dream.Explore.Build., Keone narrowed down his career interest while advancing his professional skillset. Keone is also very appreciative of the many connections he has made, especially with his peers. With Keone's hard work, competitive nature, and determined mindset, he is destined to achieve great success.

For Keone, the anthology means coming to terms with who he is and with the world around him.

## Mordechai Tinney

A self-starter and catalyst for change, Mordechai Tinney is committed to improving the lives of others and determined to succeed. Through Dream.Explore.Build., Mordechai's interest in psychology evolved into a discovery that he would like to help children develop into mentally strong and healthy adults. In the fall, Mordechai will attend Macalester College and study Psychology. He plans to study Child Psychiatry in Medical School. Mordechai's hard work and professionalism certainly haven't gone unnoticed, as he is a leader among his peers.

For Mordechai, being a part of the anthology is being a part of history. His words in this book are fundamental to who he is at this point in time. He looks forward to seeing how he develops and acts on his words in the future.

## Olivia R. Clark

With a passion for helping people live their best lives, Olivia Clark is interested in becoming a Psychotherapist. Through Dream.Explore.Build., Olivia has learned the importance of networking and building stable connections with potential employers, as well as imparting the right tools and techniques to shape her future in the field. Now a senior, Olivia plans to attend an HBCU for college.

Olivia is excited for the anthology to be shared with the world. This anthology will serve as a memorable moment in history for Olivia, and her point of view, along with her peers, will forever be etched in writing.

## Pa Kou Lee

A few years from now, Pa Kou Lee will captivate the attention of her elementary classroom. With a strong belief that every child deserves to have a great education, Pa Kou will study Early Childhood Education at Mount Mary University in the fall. She also aspires to obtain a Master's degree in Education Management. Through her internship and workshops, Pa Kou credits Dream.Explore.Build., with developing her professional skills and boosting her confidence.

For Pa Kou, participating in this anthology helped her become more aware of the feelings and experiences of others. It also served as a future reminder to treasure every moment with family and friends.

## Reginald Johnson Jr

Not only does Reginald Johnson Jr. love working with his hands, but he loves helping people fix things. For Reginald, a career in Heating and Cooling (HVAC) makes perfect sense. Entering his Senior year, Reginald has a new-found appreciation for writing and is determined to continue to grow in this skill. He looks forward to discovering new goals and building on his strengths.

For Reginald, being able to make a connection through a book with someone he's never met makes him proud of himself and his peers.

## Stephon Ricks

Driven by a passion for technology and the possibilities that lie within this innovative field, Stephon Ricks is interested in a career in Computer Science. To catapult his career, Stephon will attend Duke University in the fall. He also plans to pursue a Master's degree. Stephon credits Dream.Explore.Build. for exposing him to the life of a Computer Scientist through an internship. From that experience, Stephon connected with several professionals in the field became more versed in programming languages, and developed additional technical skills. Stephon is continuously working towards evolving in his personal and professional goals.

Stephen is excited to share his words and those of his peers with the world through this anthology. At his age, he is proud to be a published author.

## Temple Woods

What do you do when you have an interest in two career paths? For Temple Woods, you hold on to both dreams and discover everything there is to know about each career. Temple is interested in becoming an entrepreneur and/or a Child Psychologist. She holds a special place in her heart for children who are impacted by mental health issues. Next spring, Temple will enter college as a freshman. She also has plans to pursue a Master's degree. With Temple's intelligence, diligence, and attentiveness, she will excel in whatever career path she chooses to pursue.

Temple is grateful to participate in the anthology because it gives her a chance to grow her love for writing while voicing her opinion on critical topics.

## Tyrone Harper

Fascinated by the ocean and the creatures that roam the waters, Tyrone Harper is interested in pursuing a career in Marine Biology. Specifically, Tyrone looks forward to researching how animals behave and engage in the wild and discovering new life among the depths of the sea. Dream.Explore.Build. has elevated Tyrone's interviewing, presentation, and problem-solving skills. He looks forward to applying these skills as a college freshman this fall.

For Tyrone, being a part of this anthology means that he is making his voice heard and not allowing others to tell his story for him.

**Perrion Crawford (not pictured)**

Interested in becoming a Psychologist, Perrion Crawford has a bright future ahead of him. Through Dream.Explore.Build., Perrion was allowed to explore career paths while also building communication skills. Entering his senior year, Perrion plans to join the United States Army and finish out his academic year strong.

Perrion is grateful to have this experience to participate in the anthology. He looks forward to sharing the words of himself and his peers with the world.

**Jasen Moore (not pictured)**

**THE QUARANTINED TEEN** *response to*

# Life
# Interrupted

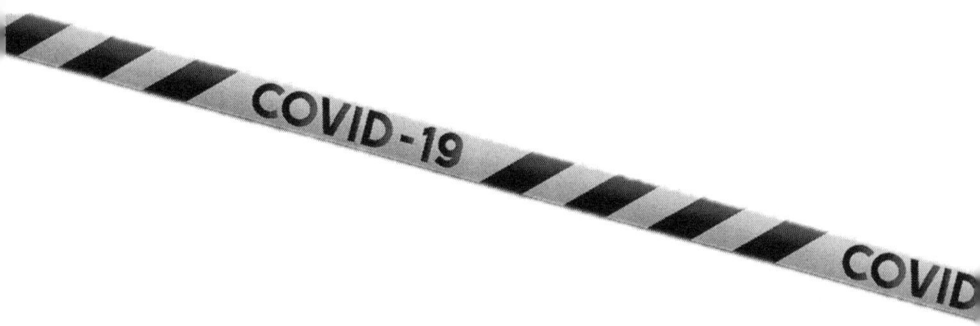
COVID-19
COVID

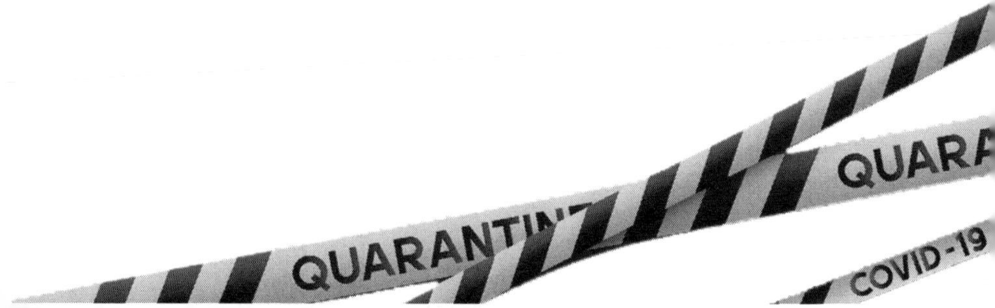
QUARANTIN
QUARA
COVID-19

## Depression

### By: Pa Kou Lee

Sitting in that room Looking down at my
feet carelessly searching for something to
cover the emptiness with hands trembling
hard trying to reach for something in the
dark but there's nothing to grab
Sitting in that room covering my ears
blocking out the sound trying hard not to listen
making sure that it does not reach my ears
yet it is hopeless, helpless
Sitting in that room silently crying inside
no sounds coming out
tears fill my eyes
struggling to push the pain away
Sitting in that room I finally realized
it was hopeless to begin with,
nothing good would come from crying
Sitting in that room
I finally let go it's time to move on time to move on

# Future Me

By: Jaylon Arms

Hey, me, from the future. You're probably reading this because you found it on the floor in your room somewhere, or you just so happened to have everything organized, and you found this on an old stack of paper. Heck, maybe you'll just glance at this and throw it away immediately after.

I know that currently, I have three goals in mind, an animator, a game designer, or a graphic designer. I have these goals in mind because they all have one value in common—freedom, specifically, the freedom to incorporate my creativity into my work. I'm committed to learning these three things in some capacity and eventually get into at least one of these careers. I want a career that's the best for me. I will stay focused and determined to finish this goal and have the end result of me being successful in mind. By this point, I learned that life is hard, and people will bring you down, but not everyone is like that. You have friends and family who are proud of you and the things you've done. Use this as motivation, use this as drive, use this to push yourself to do better.

Future me, I don't know where you'll be when you see this message. Maybe it'll just be a few days after I write this, perhaps you'll be older and a successful animator, or whatever you are in the future. Maybe you're not even reading this at all, and someone just found it drifting off in the wind. If you are reading this, though, know that you have something special, skills you've honed and practiced over the years. You have a skill that not a whole lot of people have, use that to become something great. Don't ever forget that.

## Broken Pain

By: Reginald Johnson Jr

I wanted to take her to prom and meet her Mom and Dad.
She was the one.
I was going to build my courage up to ask my crush out,
but every time I did, I seemed to punk out.
Every time I think about her, I get this weird feeling inside
I feel
*supercalifragilisticexpialidocious*
when I'm around her.
Now this pandemic came and changed my life for good.
This COVID stuff got me thinking too much.
When I texted her, the conversation was getting dry.
This relationship was fading like an old picture.
Now she gotta man. Now I'm thinking why me.
Why do I even try to push my luck?
They say there is plenty of fish in the sea.
That's the problem. She is different.
She's this coral reef bringing life to everyone she meets
she has this ecosystem about her that no fish will ever have.
She's one of a kind so it's hard to let someone go when they never leave your mind.
So Thanks COVID for letting the one get away
I thought I was going to call her wifey but I guess I'll call her friend
I guess everything has to come to an end
so I'll let my pain out
In this pen and pad broken pain on my mind now.
SOLO is the way to go right hoping this pain won't last forever I hope I meet u one
day the girl of my dreams

The Quarantined Teen response to Life Interrupted

## New Norms

By: Pa Kou Lee

Before, everything was fun
Going out with friends and having fun
Laughing crying building life together
But now
What's become of us
No friends, no interactions
But I guess that is what's become of us
During this horrified life
Living and coping in this one little house
With just family around
It's sad and cruel
It's really is, but it's not like we can help it
This is what's become of us now
Every little thing can't be helped
Life just is not the same as before
Hanging out with friends
Hugging and laughing away
All the pain of yesterday
But now
Everything is different
We will miss those days
If only we had enjoyed
Every single moment we had together
Maybe now we wouldn't' miss spending time together
I've learned things
That I wanted to share with you
But now I cannot and will not
Be able to share the knowledge

## The Quarantined Teen: Life Interrupted

Before, every single day
You and I were always together
We had each other back
But now...oh how I wish
All those times could come back
So I can tell you all my worries
I really wish I could hug you tightly
Looking back, everything was predictable
Yet I didn't care about it because
I thought it was temporary
I regret it, I really do
I should have hugged you tightly that day
But I didn't, and now it's just regret of mine
Only now I miss those moments
The talks we had while walking those crowded streets
If only I could go back in time
I would treasure those times with you
All those times, having fun together
but now, I can't do anything because
life has a different schedule for every single one of us. Before, it was fun. But now...
I miss all those times.
We are far apart with no one
to listen to my troubles and stress.
Oh...how I missed our time together...My Best Friend!

## To My Future Children

By: Temple Wood

If you are reading this, then I guess I did something right. I don't know when or how you got here, but you're here. I am 19 years old as I write this to you, and if you're shocked to be reading this, trust me I'm shocked too. Why you ask? Well, a lot of things factor into why. First, the world is harsh, and the recent turn of events has shown me it won't get any better. The fact that it's 2020 and we're still arguing about Racism and white supremacy, I don't think that shows a great sign of any real change. Well, maybe sexism will be gone, but that's a HUGE maybe. Second, building a family, marriage, and relationships, in general, doesn't have the same meaning to my generation. Two people can get married and after one year of marriage, they can "fall out of love" and get divorced.

Marriage is a flimsy word nowadays, and finding someone who has the same beliefs as me on the subject is a difficult task. The final reason and the one that I will probably struggle with the most is my own insecurities. Hopefully, you are reading this like, what insecurities, but yes, even your mother has insecurities. I have struggled with confidence and low self-esteem for what seems like forever. Not because I don't have a loving family or even great people around me, but at this point, I have gotten comfortable being insecure about myself, and I know that no one can change that but me. Since you're reading this, then I did do something right. I didn't let my assumptions about the world and my fear of not finding a suitable husband or my own myself stop me from bringing you into the world. I hope you have a more positive look on life than me. I hope me and your father's marriage is like the example I had on what marriage is supposed to look like. Most of all, I hope that by the time we meet, I'm someone you know you can rely on and someone you feel comfortable enough to talk to about anything and everything. Even though I haven't met you yet, I think I can speak for the future Temple and say that I love you unconditionally and when I make mistakes as a parent, try not to hold it against me, just learn from them.

Love,

19-year-old me

# Extra

### By: Anisha Prather

Split I cannot sit,
my mind stems from my grip
A grip brought to reality,
not being heard would be my fatality

Hear me now or hear me not,
I wonder if you see the big plot
The plot in our mentality,
please let's bring out some formality

# Don't Forget Me

### By: Pa Kou Lee

Grey hair
Wrinkle face
Smiling with everything that I have
Saying words of wisdom
To always remember the energetic me
Burn the sweet voice of mine in your head
Shed your tears but not much
Save some for your future to come
For I am old and can not
Go farther than one step
Grey hair
Wrinkle face
Always smiling towards the end
Don't forget me
Remembering that there are times that are going to be hard
It's going to be long
But in a blink of an eye
Time will rush me to hurry up
And here I am on my deathbed
Whispering wisdom words
To you to pass along the way
And slowly closing my eyes
I'll be waiting on the other side
One day you'll meet me once again
So it is only goodbye for now
Remember that I will always be waiting on the other side for you

# Collection of the Things Missed Out On

By: Mordechai Tinney

The first day of class,
being dropped off and retreating,
finding solace in loneliness because I was left alone,
no one wants to leave their parents in K5,
now they may not have to,
may not have to break out of their shell
to continue their deep dependence on a parent's presence.

A celebration so grand,
at least of the ones I've seen before,
as I walk on stage to stand,
to be celebrated some more,
1st-grade graduation is novel,
and something more novel takes its place

Middle School
the time of discovery and friendship,
learning who I am and where I belong,
a challenging time with testy friends,
relationships are born and shattered with ease,
life becomes complicated,
much too complicated when it's all done from home.

A new me,
created in each and every instance,
the future will be,
brought to a crawl
Dependent on the novel,
that all of us are a part of.

## Future Seniors

By: Temple Woods

I'm sorry. I am sorry you have to grow up this way. For me, growing up is nerve-racking. I am taught next to nothing in school about preparing for living on my own, like budgeting and doing taxes. I am given an adult-like decision to figure out what career to do for the rest of my life. Still, at the same time being told that "you're young, you'll figure it out eventually", which to me is like guessing on a test and hoping I got the right answer, and it's NOT multiple choice. Spending 12 years in schools hoping that eventually, I would figure it out, but still not knowing at the age of 19, and that was before the pandemic. But you, you may not get that luxury of enjoying your last year of school, or as I would like to call it your last year of "youth". I had the choice of going to prom, which was no by the way, but you may not get that choice.

I apologize for the mistakes that this country has made that the event you were looking forward to, stripped from you. That the stress, long nights, pressures from society and parents, the work-hard and time you spent to graduate and walk across that stage, taken from you. You are the ones that are suffering the most from these drastic turn of events. I hope this doesn't stop you from accomplishing your dreams, and you don't waste too much time trying to figure it out from here.

Sincerely,

A 2020 Graduate

# Halted

By: Keone Westfall

Halted, as we watch from our windows
as the gentle wind blows
a plastic bag down the street,
a street that once was alive
now looking so barren but,
inside I feel trapped
inside I look back
inside my mind is racing
inside I am bored
inside my heart is sore
inside, I don't want to do this anymore
I want to go outside
I want to go on vacation
I want to walk across the stage,
I want this to be a dream
because my dream already seemed so far
yet the end of this is so far, out of reach,
but alas this won't happen because for now we are just, halted

*The Quarantined Teen response to Life Interrupted*

# Fear

By: Pa Kou Lee

I closed my eyes very tightly
clutching my blanket and trying to hide from her.
My heart beat faster than my head could think
She's scary but I don't want to hear her me
My heart thumps hard
I hope she doesn't hear my heart thumping loud
I hope I can have at least a good night sleep
I desire not to see her I really do
But she thinks otherwise
My body is frozen
Still wishing that she can let me sleep tonight
Yet now I wait, and with that, she will let me have one good night
Without being scared and tired
She stares at me with that hollow eye
Looking at my every step
She stares at me and it creeps me out
No words can describe such devilishness
That she shows me
It's scary, I am
Horrified
Petrified
Eerie
She
Stares
At me
I close my eyes very tightly
Clutching my blanket
Trying to hide from her

## The Quarantined Teen: Life Interrupted

She yanked my blanket
And I wake up with sweat on my face
So glad
It was just a dream
That I can wake up from

*The Quarantined Teen response to Life Interrupted*

# Shaking

By: Reginald Johnson Jr

Overthinking every time I think about this subject
I step forward my body gets tense like tectonic plates
and I get stuck
and my heart starts to race
and the pressure builds up
and when I open up my mouth
it will cause an earthquake which made a whole lot of pain
I want to get better so
I'm trying to write this feeling away
but every time
I put the pen on the pad
my hand gets sweaty
It's like my body is telling me
this is more than a poem or a song
this is a movie
so you got to be strong as a rock
but still have heart
I can't get out of my own head
it's like I'm trapped in the dark
every time I try to get out and move forward the room starts to quake, I feel uneasy
I feel like I'm going to fall
and the room keeps quaking
and I don't know when it will end
I hope I can pretend
to be ok
smiling through the pain
I hope they won't see my pain
because if I talk it will hurt
Pushing people away is the only way to go

## The Quarantined Teen: Life Interrupted

because I don't want to hurt anyone like I'm hurt,
so I'm quivering at the fact
I don't want my people or my friends to see me like this
at my lowest point
and the room walls are only getting taller
and closer
and it's getting hard to breath
trying to yell for help
but they won't see my pain through my pride,
the only way they will really see me
is if I try to commit suicide.
Is that the only way to go,
seeing yo own dead body hanging from the ceiling,
some stories never end like you think
imagine dying over the fact you was afraid to speak
Shaking in fear to show your personality.

## A Collective Voice

As I reflect on the experience of working with the youth of Lead2Change, the word *floored* is the only way I can describe the amount of wisdom that overwhelmed me, emulating from these young minds.

With each workshop, their words captured emotions, thoughts, and experiences that allowed me a glimpse into their world amid this pandemic of Racism and COVID-19.

We met virtually over zoom and in our chat room there were so many what I like to call "leftover words, and leftover thoughts." I could not just leave dangling there. I knew I had to capture them somewhere, here.

I'd like to invite you to encounter the raw emotions and expressions of the Quarantined Teen, Life Interrupted. The next poem was assembled using real-time responses during our summer 2020 Youth AuthorLab writing experience.

Enjoy.

– Liz Luckett

# Emotions

Fear mad anxious sadness
emotions that I knew existed
but somehow in this sad twisted reality
they seem to plague me
happy is what I choose among the chaos
frustrated that there are times I must admit
it eludes me and frustration takes its place
I am tired of sitting home waiting
Hopeless antidotes of agitated dreams seem to all converge into disappointment
Agitated I relax and ask
What do you mean love isn't a feeling
Love is a thing?
Envious that love gets to evade emotion
Disgusted and impatient I wait until
Irritation turns into
Dare I say it
Energy, energetic sensations of contentment
seem to overwhelm me
creativity starts to persuade me
through sleepy eyes, that chaos
no matter how chaotic
will give way to innovative...occurrences of peace

- Liz Luckett

**THE QUARANTINED TEEN**
# Journal Prompts

The youth of the Summer 2020 Lead2Change Cohort prepared journal prompts to encourage our readers to explore their Life Interrupted. We encourage youth and adults to take time and journal reflections around the health and heart crisis of 2020. We learned that writing is a way to express our emotions and can have a positive impact on our mental health. Enjoy the prompts below and record your reflections on this unforgettable moment in history.

### Perrion Crawford

- Does racism/COVID make you feel neglected, alone, left out?
- Have you ever witnessed someone being discriminated against? If so, how did it make you feel? What was the situation?
- If you had the power to take one away, which would it be, COVID 19 or Racism? Why did you choose that one?

### Olivia R. Clark

- Did you think Racism exists in your family?
- What will you tell your future kids/grandkids about the year 2020?

### Darriunna Cole

- Have you ever isolated yourself?
- How has your life changed as a result of COVID 19?

### Dianyeliz Garcia

- Have you addressed your own racial biases against other people, whether they are people of color or white?
- Name five people you know who have been affected by COVID or Racism and write how you will support them.

### Pa Kou Lee

- Write a letter to yourself in the future.

### Keone Westfall

- Why do you think Racism has been allowed to grow?

### Mordechai Tinney

- Write about an experience in which you have had to challenge the belief of a family member. How did you feel?
- Write a response to a piece in the book.

### Anisha Prather

- What new things will you give to the world after COVID 19 is over?
- Why can't everyone see each other's side peacefully?

**Stephon Ricks**

- What did you do inside the home during quarantine times?
- Do you believe the riots and raids were justified?

**Temple Woods**

- What are some positive aspects of your life right now since the pandemic started?

**Jacqueline Oliva-Jacobo**

- If Racism was a person, how would they look / what would they act like?
- Do you believe Racism will still be an issue 20 years from now? Explain why or why not

## Our Parting Words

May our voices forever be captured in time

   and may our words forever hold a place

      in your heart

         to one day become

           a distant memory

              of a Quarantined Teen

                 Life Interrupted

## About Lead2Change

Lead2Change is a career-readiness organization that engages young people in leadership opportunities and equips them with essential tools to be successful in college, their career and the community. Young people who experience our programming enter the post-secondary world confident and clear about their career interests and their position in the global workforce.

For more information on how to engage with Lead2Change, please visit our website at www.lead2changeinc.org.